'1001 Further Writing Prompts

For Generating Ideas'

By Sarah Hindmarsh

'1001 Writing Further Prompts For Generating Ideas'
by Sarah Hindmarsh

First published 2017

1) Writing 2) Non-Fiction

Contents

Preface

This is the third in the '1001 Writing Prompts for Generating Ideas' series. I hope all my readers are finding the books useful. I love having so many ideas floating about in my head that I can share 1001 at a time with other writers to help them generate ideas of their own. These books are actually great fun to write but I think this might well be the last in this series. I have more ideas for books to help writers, beginners and more experienced alike, in different ways.

As always these prompts contain no obscenities or graphic content, and are suitable for writers of all ages. Use them as you will, dive in and try all 1001 if you really feel inspired. As with all collections of writing prompts there will be some that speak to you and some that don't particularly ignite any spark. I have tried to include a selection of prompts that can be used by writers of a variety of genres of short fiction and even some that may be useful to poets.

Above all I wish you productivity and enjoyment with your writing.

Chapter 1 – What If?

Sometimes all it takes to spark the imagination is a scenario that speaks to the possibilities inside your head. It can be something very small that isn't quite what it seems or something huge that would change the world completely. Of course something small could also change the world completely. That's the beauty of being a writer, even that shoe that your dog chewed up could be important to a story. Take these prompts and see what ten minutes of free writing about them produces. Ask yourself What If? Perhaps you'll end up with a story, maybe a poem, maybe something else entirely. That part is up to you.

1)   Doors led to other worlds
2)   Only girls went to school
3)   Witches were real
4)   Horses could smell treasure
5)   A unicorn appeared in your garden
6)   Inspiration was an actual person who had to hit you
7)   All the fruit in the world turned into oranges
8)   A five year old was running the world
9)   You were a ghost
10) The smell of flowers was toxic
11) Spoons were illegal
12) Leather was made from human skin
13) Oxygen was really poisoning us
14) Alarms went off when someone told a secret
15) Shoes were intelligent
16) Eggs were the only food in the world
17) The earth stopped spinning on its axis
18) Cats were telepathic

19) Laughing was a criminal offence publishable by
    death
20) Alcohol made people smarter
21) All restaurants were at the top of mountains
22) Someone found the garden of Eden
23) Holidays meant you had to stay in bed
24) Men vanished
25) Convicts were still sent to Australia
26) People had gardens on their roofs
27) Everyone forgot how to read
28) Santa's elves went on strike
29) Grass had stings
30) Your scissors could talk
31) Winning the lottery meant you were going to die
    in a year
32) Nobody ever apologised
33) Butterflies could predict the future
34) God sent messages by carrier pigeon
35) Bullets contained flower petals
36) All the fish jumped out of the sea
37) Blackberries were used as currency
38) Learning salsa dancing was compulsory
39) Smoking improved your health
40) Everyone lived to 1000
41) Someone beat Death at chess
42) Bacteria were really tiny aliens
43) All windows had burglar bars
44) There were no speed limits
45) All the air con units in the world broke at
    once
46) Everyone had to live at the south pole
47) Pens would only work if you paid them a
    compliment
48) Houses were built by gnomes
49) Stars were really giant fireflies
50) All words starting with S were banned

51) Elections were decided by an IQ test
52) Asparagus grew everywhere instead of grass
53) Sculptures could come to life
54) Rabbits hated carrots
55) Icecream was warm
56) Everything green disappeared
57) Bath Bombs really exploded
58) Death died
59) Ladybirds and spiders were at war
60) The bus was late
61) You forgot the clocks had changed
62) Someone stopped to help a lost dog
63) Your car was blocked in by an ambulance
64) You slipped into an alternate reality
65) A maniac kidnapped someone
66) Your sat nav tried to drown you in a river
67) Your sat nav succeeded in drowning you in a river
68) A guinea pig escaped
69) Someone was called into work as an emergency
70) You didn't want to go somewhere
71) You got lost in a corn maize
72) Someone forgot what day it was
73) Someone sent a letter bomb to Santa Claus
74) There was a ghost in your new home
75) Someone was obsessed with a model on an advert
76) You were accidentally set up with your ex
77) You were a week early for a job interview
78) Granny got a new pet
79) A woman didn't recognise her husband
80) Your date turned out to be an escaped mental patient
81) Grandad got drunk
82) Nobody showed up to a party
83) You could only communicate with someone by cave painting

84) Only people who were good at sports were
    allowed to have children
85) You lost your licence if you crashed your car
86) It was possible to fall off the edge of the
    world
87) Someone had shoes stitched with unicorn hair
88) You got caught in a civil war
89) Chemistry experiments produced magic potions
90) You could travel through time by looking at
    pictures
91) A member of your family murdered someone
92) You were about to marry someone you knew you
    didn't love
93) Your best friend won the lottery
94) You discovered a new species of animal that
    turned out to be an alien
95) A small child went missing on a run-down
    housing estate
96) The light didn't turn on when you hit the
    switch
97) an accountant decided to be an actor
98) You were invisible for just two hours
99) The police shot someone who was innocent
100) You were blindfolded and led through the woods

Chapter 2 – What's My Story?

Sometimes a story can be inspired not by a scenario but by an unusual character. Some of the best stories come from a character getting inside a writer's head and refusing to be ignored. I've come up with some bizarre and some wonderful characters for your to write about. Have a look at the brief descriptions below and ask yourself if any of those characters are trying to tell you their stories.

101) Marjorie, who fairies are afraid of
102) Max, who should never have been in the
     defendant's seat in the first place
103) Rowan who was following her own shadow
104) Ali who just wants to be a pirate
105) Carrie, who owns thirty seven cats
106) Eloise who is standing on the edge of a cliff
107) Cameron who is permanently stuck in the friend
     zone
108) Maria who is always the problem
109) Giovanni who never uses his real name
110) Debbie who built a library in her basement
111) Aston who wants to be a ballet dancer
112) Janice a painter who lives in Paris
113) Ethan who is obsessed with Halloween
114) Saffron who always pays it forward
115) Martin who chews his lip when he's lying
116) Austin who is restoring an old house
117) Jessie who is always described by her team as a
     'pocket rocket'
118) Clive who hasn't seen his son in 10 years
119) Doris who collects hairbrushes
120) Jonny who lives in an abandoned church

121) Cadence who used to be a world champion
122) Bruno who speaks to the dead
123) Shirley who likes everything old fashioned
124) Brian who hasn't left his house in a year
125) Claudia who loves fire
126) Jackson who always asks for seconds
127) Emily who believes in everyone but herself
128) Horatio who has twelve guitars
129) Mollie who cries all the time
130) Firdaus who always sleeps through his alarm
131) Topaz who can't remember if she's alive or dead
132) Mason who only wears red or blue
133) Freya who has the worst haircut in the entire
     school
134) Callan who used to be a risk consultant
135) Jack who hates spinach, even though he's never
     eaten it
136) Rose who didn't want to get up this morning
137) James who stayed at home to read a book
138) Mariam who got a flat tyre yesterday
139) George who tells everyone he was abducted by
     aliens
140) Alice who really was abducted by aliens
141) Sam who doesn't realise his best friend is in
     love with him
142) Susie who can't stand to be single
143) Rhodi who runs a wildlife safari business
144) Pandora who makes earrings shaped like boxes
145) Aaron who invented tomatoes
146) Harley who drives it like he stole it
147) Annabel who can't drive but runs a driving
     school
148) Olivier who has never won anything in his life
149) Katherine who lives to play rugby
150) Isaac who loves robots
151) Mia who trains guide dogs

152) Jenson who sponsors twenty snow leopards
153) Cara who plays over thirty musical instruments
154) Fabian who has never seen a Disney movie
155) Amie who spends all her free time at the local
     stables
156) Euan who wants to get his squad back together
157) Violet who can't take a picture without a
     filter
158) Owen who didn't want to go
159) Maisie who can't stop drinking tea
160) Jasper who is trying to take the perfect photo
161) Shannon who has never had a cold
162) Mickey who eats mashed potatoes with every meal
163) Julia who loves dogs but is allergic to them
164) Ray who lives in his car
165) Jasmine who thinks she has a fairy godmother
166) Benjamin whose wife is much more attractive
     than him
167) Connie who tells everyone her mother is dead
168) Cody who has failed every exam he has ever
     taken
169) Glitter who lives in an eco-friendly house
170) Grady who has difficulty saying no
171) Diana who talks to her pot plants
172) Levi who won't take off his wedding ring
173) Trey who tells lots of little white lies
174) Tamara who is always spending too much money
175) Gary whose family don't know he is joining the
     army
176) Carlie who walks dogs for a living
177) Jacques who made millions in the dot com boom
178) Michelle who is a customs officer
179) Patrick who is not a very good listener
180) Darcy who never wanted children
181) Devin who always wears short - even in winter
182) Catriona who is having counselling

183) Paul who just had a new knee
184) Sunita who sings her children to sleep every
    night
185) Kristian who washes his hair in beer
186) Jemma who only wears batman t-shirts
187) Toby who wears glasses even though he doesn't
    need them
188) Donna who has over 100 stuffed unicorns
189) Gordon who likes to make an entrance
190) Olivia who has an imaginary friend
191) Ian who actually has a pocket watch
192) Kasia who types with one finger
193) Shane who won't wear the same pair of jeans two
    days running
194) Aoife who believes in the tooth fairy
195) Taran who always has to touch everything
196) Niamh who carries everything bar the kitchen
    sink in their handbag
197) Connor who is extremely superstitious
198) Abigail who rearranges her furniture every day
199) Blake who treats everyone he meets as a friend
200) Dylan who is addicted to texting

Chapter 3 - Answer Me This!

A great story starts with a great hook, a question the reader will want to find an answer to. If the only way they can find the answer to that question is to keep reading then that is exactly what they will do. In this chapter I pose a hundred questions to intrigue writers and readers alike. If you can answer these questions then you might just have a story worth writing! Try writing the question in the middle of a blank page and adding ideas for answers as a spider diagram. These questions are also excellent discussion questions for creative writing classes, writing groups and school lessons. Once you have an answer to the question you are happy with build a story or a narrative poem around it. Some of the questions are serious, others are frankly absurd - but that's half the fun!

201) Why would anyone try to assassinate the easter bunny?
202) Why doesn't a teenager own a mobile phone?
203) How does dinner turn into murder?
204) Why wait until next year?
205) Why won't your character drive a car?
206) Why is someone afraid of the rain?
207) Why did someone have to pass a law against eating live goldfish?
208) What is the world coming to?
209) Why did the sky turn red?
210) If all the world's a stage, where does the audience sit?
211) Who broke the remote control?
212) Where did Noah keep the woodpeckers?
213) Who changes the bags on the vacuum of space?

214) Why do banks chain pens to the counter?
215) Why has a psychic never won the lottery?
216) Why isn't cat food mouse flavoured?
217) What happened to Mr Jones from number 11?
218) Who paints the spots on ladybirds?
219) Why would a paramedic refuse to help someone?
220) Why is there an elephant in central park?
221) Why didn't you turn up for work today?
222) Why is the house on the corner empty?
223) What happened to the pink balloon?
224) Why was she outside in a thunderstorm?
225) Why aren't there any photos of someone?
226) How did a spider get stuck in its own web?
227) When will the world end?
228) How did a crow learn to talk?
229) Why doesn't the escalator work?
230) Why is the garden overgrown?
231) Why can't you get through that door?
232) Why is the window always open?
233) Why did the fish die?
234) Where did the fur coats come from?
235) How do you fix the unfixable?
236) Why would someone who loves history do a degree
    in physics?
237) Why was he dreading the visitors?
238) How do you make an egg explode?
239) What is the camel wishing for?
240) Why give your house keys to a stranger?
241) What are you frantically looking for?
242) Why was there a knock at the door?
243) Why was there Sushi for dessert?
244) Why can't you remember his name?
245) Why does my eye twitch?
246) Why doesn't she change the clocks?
247) Why has Halloween been moved to June?
248) Why can't she get a job?

249) Why is he asleep in the middle of the day?
250) Why is the internet suddenly so slow?
251) Why isn't youtube working?
252) Why would someone block you?
253) Why would someone want to work in retail?
254) Why would you need a brain scan?
255) Why would someone not enter a plea?
256) Why are they getting divorced?
257) Why is she always cold?
258) Why is gin good for you?
259) Why did she lie to you?
260) Why are they in jail?
261) Why is he jumping off a bridge?
262) Why does Mummy drink?
263) Why is it dangerous not to be normal?
264) Why is this volunteer important?
265) Why are there fireworks tonight?
266) Why did the relationship fail?
267) Why is Zeus angry?
268) How will the mountain die?
269) What are they demolishing?
270) What did he do in the shadows?
271) What did Vikings eat?
272) What made him apply for that position?
273) What made the mad king mad?
274) Who made the moon?
275) Why is he running?
276) Why did they let the dogs out?
277) When will they see each other again?
278) What was that noise?
279) Why was the train delayed?
280) How did she get a concussion?
281) Why won't there be a Christmas this year?
282) What happened to Japan?
283) Why is there blood on your hands?
284) What do the green stars mean?

285) Why is the temperature dropping?
286) What made the earth move?
287) Why was the holiday cancelled?
288) Why didn't he want to see his father?
289) Why can I see whales?
290) Why were the monsters under the bed?
291) What happened on Monday?
292) How does she know what the ocean tastes like?
293) What could make a vampire afraid?
294) Why is there literally a skeleton in the
     closet?
295) What caused the traffic jam?
296) How did they get on the spaceship?
297) How did the sheep get out?
298) Why did nobody win the race?
299) Why is there a panda wearing a bathrobe?
300) Why can't she take a compliment?

Chapter 4 – Dear Allie

Agony aunts get all kinds of fabulous inspiration for stories. People write to them and spill all their problems into their inboxes. The agony aunt pages of women's magazines can be a treasure trove of sob stories, love stories, bad luck stories and tortured souls. The next 100 prompts are samples of some of the things that can found in these columns all gathered into one place so you don't need to trawl through hundreds of magazines. All these people are obviously made up (some more obviously than others) but their struggles represent real opportunities for story gold! You could think about how they might solve the problem, how they go into the situation in the first place, what happens if they snap under the pressure, whether the problem is really all in their head. There are so many ways you could take these prompts and turn them into something unique. I have no idea who Allie is – but she's my fictional agony aunt for now – so Dear Allie …

301) I think my husband might be an alien!
302) I fancy my boyfriend's brother
303) My family don't think I can sing but I'm
     desperate to be a pop star
304) I'm in love with my teacher, and I think she
     loves me too
305) I puked at prom
306) I haven't spoken to my mother in twenty years
     and now she's dying
307) My siblings hate me because I stole my sister's
     husband

308) My boyfriend spends more time in the pub with
     the boys than with me
309) I caught my husband wearing my underwear
310) My friends all hate my new partner and I don't
     understand why
311) I fell out with my best friend over a holiday
312) My mum grounded me - I'm twenty five!
313) I talk to my boyfriend's chest hair
314) I feel like I've lost touch with everyone and I
     don't know how to fix it
315) Going to work gives me panic attacks
316) My friend is a complete know it all - but he's
     always wrong
317) I want kids but my boyfriend doesn't
318) How do I tell my pregnant girlfriend I'm gene
     positive for Huntingtons disease?
319) How do I get my friend to stop inviting herself
     to events where she isn't welcome?
320) My colleague keeps cramping my style with the
     boys in the office
321) My son hasn't ever had a girlfriend, how do I
     help him find love?
322) He won't leave his wife and I'm getting fed up!
323) I hate my girlfriend's hair style but she won't
     change it
324) The other kids at school laugh at me because I
     can't afford nice clothes
325) I think one of my colleagues is stealing from
     our boss
326) I have to choose my A levels this year and I
     don't know what to choose
327) How do I stop my siblings borrowing my clothes?
328) My friend seems miserable and I'm worried but
     she won't tell me what's wrong
329) I kissed my best friend and now she won't speak
     to me

330) My parents keep asking when I'm having kids –
     how do I tell them I don't want any?
331) I married the wrong man
332) My teenage daughter won't leave her room
333) I've had dates with three different guys this
     month – they ALL stood me up
334) What should I get my vegan friend for
     Christmas? – I give everyone else chocolates
335) How do I get my girlfriend to stop filling the
     house with unicorn statues?
336) I think my wife is cheating on me
337) My boyfriend won't get rid of his star trek
     costumes
338) I think I'm in love with my house plant
339) I really want to be abducted by aliens
340) My housemate is obsessed with becoming a
     wrestler
341) I'm worried my girlfriend might be a serial
     killer
342) My boyfriend's toe nails keep growing after he
     cuts them
343) I blew three million after winning the lottery
344) My mum's dog attacked the postman
345) How do I tell my mum I've decided to be a
     stripper?
346) I don't want to quit my degree to look after my
     mum but my brother won't help
347) My boyfriend asked me to move in but my lease
     isn't up for another 6 months
348) I think my cat is plotting to take over the
     world
349) I'm sure I saw my garden gnomes moving last
     night
350) My daughter refuses to pay attention to one of
     her twin sons
351) I've lost my job and can't bear to tell my wife

352) My girlfriend wants me to get a tattoo of her
     name
353) How do I get my dad to stop smoking weed?
354) My girlfriend keeps spending all my money
355) My friends won't take my advice about herbal
     remedies
356) I'm embarrassed by my partner's table manners
357) I've never kissed anyone and I'm worried I
     won't know how
358) My partner left me because I'm "too middle
     class"
359) My thirteen year old daughter is pregnant
360) My mother in law keeps interfering in our
     marriage
361) My partner left me for my sister
362) Housemate's stinky cheese is ruining my life
363) How do I come out to my sheep farming family as
     vegan?
364) My forty year old son still lives with me - how
     do I kick him out?
365) I hate my girlfriend's cat
366) My three year old speaks French - and we don't
     know how he learned it
367) I lost my memory and don't know who I'm married
     to
368) I think my boss is in league with the devil
369) I think there's a bat colony living in my roof
370) My girlfriend wants to get married in Barbados
     but I'm terrified of flying
371) My unicorn won't stop stabbing people I don't
     like
372) I'm worried I might be dead
373) My boyfriend proposed but I'm still in love
     with someone else
374) I broke the bro code

375) I didn't realise my girlfriend was drinking
     until one night she came home sober
376) I joined the navy to see the world - the world
     sucks, I want out
377) I'm having an affair with my boss
378) I asked someone out for a dare but now I really
     like them
379) I can't choose which of my 11 brothers should
     be my best man
380) How do I help my friend who's being abused by
     her parents?
381) My mum won't stop hoarding empty bottles
382) Help! My husband joined a cult
383) There's a ghost living in the walls of my house
384) My gorgeous friend has no idea I'm in love with
     her
385) I'm twenty grand in debt to a loan shark
386) Babysitter dropped my toddler down the stairs
387) I hate the cold but my husband won't let me
     turn up the heating
388) I hate all four of my kids
389) How do I tell Mum it was me that burned down
     the house?
390) Why won't my owl deliver letters to my friends?
391) My imaginary friend cut off my sister's hair
392) My neighbour keeps mowing my lawn
393) I think my guardian angel died
394) I poisoned half the neighbourhood with out of
     date Halloween candy
395) My horse kicked over a gravestone
396) I think my neighbour's baby is being neglected
397) Help! My fairy godmother turned evil
398) My gym buddy abandoned me and now I'm getting
     fat
399) Mum tidied my room and now I can't find
     anything!

400) Strangers turned up to my party and trashed my
     house

Chapter 5 – Written in the Stars

Another fabulous resource found in magazines and newspapers is the star signs section. The best thing about these sections is that they are usually so vague that they can apply to almost anything so there's plenty of room for your imagination to work. Imagine one of the following prompts was the star sign for a character for the coming week. In what ways might these predictions manifest in their lives? How would they cope with them? You may like to start with a spider diagram to explore the various ways these predictions could affect someone until you find a scenario you're happy with.

401) You will meet someone who will make a big difference in your life
402) This might be a good time to think about that important financial decision you've been putting off
403) A development in your social life leads to an exciting opportunity
404) A friend could be in need of a little TLC this week
405) An old argument will resurface around the full moon, now might be the time to resolve it
406) Issues with older members of the family are at the forefront of your mind over the coming week
407) A pressing work problem could turn into a golden opportunity
408) Your love life might take a hit early this week but hang in there for better later on
409) Now is the time to take steps towards that ambition you've been hiding for a while

410) You feel a strong need for liberation this
     week, make sure you figure out what it is that
     is really holding you back
411) Stop telling yourself the world will fall apart
     without you, it's time to take a break from
     certain high stress activities
412) This week should sort out a love dilemma
413) This week is the perfect time to reconnect with
     an old friend, just make sure you pick the
     right one
414) If you're prepared to move out of your comfort
     zone your living situation could be really
     looking up this week
415) A dream you had recently will prove to be
     significant this week
416) You'll be recognised for something you've been
     working on for a while this week
417) Be yourself when attempting to impress someone
     important this week
418) A journey beckons for you this week
419) Venus will be pressing home her work/life
     balance agenda this week
420) You'll experience a eureka moment for a long
     term problem this week
421) If you don't put yourself first this week the
     consequences could be disastrous
422) You've been putting in the effort at work for a
     while now and the fruits of your labour are
     about to be revealed
423) Allow yourself to dream this week, but be
     careful not to get carried away and forget
     about something basic
424) Someone has a "my way or the highway" attitude
     this week, don't let them drag you down with
     them when it backfires

425) You'll gain insight into a pressing family
     matter this week
426) Don't be surprised if someone from your past
     puts in an appearance this week
427) If money is holding you back then look for the
     obvious way to fix that
428) You'll have to face your fears this week,
     there's no chance of running and hiding
429) An inappropriate romantic interest rears their
     head this week
430) You'll need all your strength to resist
     temptation this week
431) Trust your gut when it comes to someone who
     doesn't deserve a second chance this week
432) Your emotions could get the better of you at
     work this week
433) This week holds a pivotal moment for your love
     life, if you can recognise it.
434) A childhood wound will make its presence felt
     this week
435) You'll have the opportunity to stand up to
     someone this week
436) This week holds an intense adrenalin rush for
     your inner competitor
437) The weather will be important for some of your
     endeavours this week
438) There's a big upheaval at home ahead
439) Someone has a shock announcement this week
440) You're doing the right thing for the wrong
     reason, make sure it doesn't come back to bite
     you
441) This week sees karma back on your side
442) You've got a super energy boost, it's the
     perfect time to join the gym or take up a new
     hobby

443) Try not to gloat when you prove someone wrong
     this week
444) A travel delay could prove significant this
     week
445) Animals are causing havoc this week, the only
     way to cope is to embrace the madness
446) You'll have an opportunity to bury the hatchet
     coming up
447) Being careful about communication could lead to
     exciting events this week
448) Your personal needs will clash with a loved
     one's this week
449) Don't jump in to the water too quickly this
     week, the currents are stronger than they seem
     to be
450) You'll need a close bond with someone to get
     through a trauma at home this week
451) Mother nature is taking a stab at you this week
452) A toxic relationship is going to come to light
     this week, take the opportunity to get rid of
     the one causing you problems
453) If you don't know the origin of that rumour
     that's been bothering you look a little closer
     to home
454) A hunch will pay off this week
455) Don't be taken in by someone's superficial
     charm
456) An addiction will get in the way of a lucrative
     opportunity this week
457) This week is the start of a massive change at
     work
458) A past regret will reveal itself as a useful
     learning experience this week
459) If you can't think of a solution to a problem
     this week try taking a walk

460) An unexpected love interest could emerge this
     week - whether you want it to or not
461) The tug of the past will draw you into conflict
     this week
462) A secret will be unearthed towards the end of
     the week. Pay attention.
463) Someone will reveal their true colours this
     week, and you aren't going to like them
464) A purchase will prove to be more than you
     bargained for
465) It's time to ditch the comfort blanket and take
     the leap. You can do it!
466) Somebody's missing from your social circle this
     week, I'd check on them if I were you
467) That crazy idea you had a while ago doesn't
     seem so crazy this week
468) Accommodation issues are about to come to a
     head
469) Someone's pushing their luck this week, is it
     worth pushing back?
470) Watch out for Granddad (yours or someone
     else's!)
471) Hope you're feeling athletic this week, you're
     going to need to be
472) A friend is worth their weight in gold this
     week when your family are demanding too much
     from you
473) Your self-preservation instinct is in overdrive
     this week, and it needs to be
474) I'd avoid the woods this week if I were you
475) Holiday plans may be going awry but there's a
     light at the end of the tunnel
476) Be careful not to knock on the wrong door this
     week
477) Somebody has an exciting obsession - be careful
     not to get drawn in

478) The universe is about to send you a sign
regarding your career goals
479) There's an unexpected new friendship in the
offing this week
480) This week's new moon is the perfect opportunity
for you to conjure up your desires
481) There'll be a separation heralding permanent
change this week
482) You'll have persuasive super powers this week,
use them wisely
483) Technology is your best friend this week
484) Your adventurous side is growing teeth this
week
485) There'll be no more excuses for something
you've been putting off for a while this week
486) You've got the keys to the door, this week is
the time to unlock it
487) This week could be the time to consider an
important purchase
488) There's instability at home this week, with an
unexpected cause
489) Someone is going to test your loyalty in the
coming days
490) You're about to have an amazing creative idea,
be sure you make the most of it
491) There's not much of that peace and quiet you
wanted around this week
492) An old demon is stalking your thoughts this
week
493) An argument is in the offing this week, best to
get it over with
494) Your love life will go through a rebirth in the
coming weeks
495) You'll have to start something all over again
this week

496) There's some unexpected game-changing support
     coming your way this week
497) Words can work magic so use them to your
     advantage this week
498) There's an important meeting coming up this
     week, make sure it's not a disaster
499) You need to learn something this week, but it's
     not entirely clear what
500) The green eyed monster is rearing his ugly
     head, and he won't be easy to slay

Chapter 6 – Sentence Starters

An old favourite returns for this edition of 1001 Writing Prompts. Sentence starters are designed to get the creative juices flowing by prompting you to first complete the sentence, and then to continue writing. Set your timers for five minutes, ten minutes, or however long you think you can comfortably write without lifting your pen from the paper. Ready, set, go …

501) If only I had gone another way …
502) Somebody had to tell her …
503) Her shadow was right …
504) Crash! The mast hit the deck …
505) The journey took nearly three years …
506) Year after year the crops failed …
507) The heat grew so strong it scorched the wings of the bees …
508) I had to concentrate hard to see through the magic …
509) The basket under the table started to move …
510) I'd seen this fairy a dozen times before …
511) His shoes were made of real alligator skins …
512) It was sometime after two when the car pulled up …
513) We were at the bar when the trouble started …
514) I lead the resistance around here …
515) We grew up together in Newcastle upon Tyne …
516) It never hurts to have a pretty girl at the bar …
517) I got the feeling he was covering for his buddy …
518) The maid was half the problem …

519) I had a great wardrobe - for someone 40lbs
     lighter than me …
520) Every night is the same dream …
521) Tree tops poked above the mist as if they were
     floating …
522) I heard the door open and he was gone …
523) The timeline was a little unclear …
524) After less than a minute he snapped the book
     shut …
525) I had completely forgotten the clocks had
     changed …
526) He walked the same way to work every day …
527) I don't think they'd ever seen mud before …
528) The jury's verdict echoed round the room …
529) It was a good thing they'd forgotten about the
     back room …
530) We had already agreed not to press charges …
531) It sounded like she wanted to help …
532) It was as though they knew we would be there …
533) I wanted nothing more than to get out of there
     …
534) It was only six months ago …
535) They did the same thing every weekend …
536) They must have seen her coming …
537) The guy was no friend of mine …
538) Some people just seem to like trouble …
539) I could have talked to her again …
540) It took all night to find out the truth …
541) There were heavy footsteps heading for the door
     …
542) The dead girl's mother raised her head …
543) My stomach flipped as I breathed in her perfume
     …
544) The smell of newly cut hay hit my nostrils …
545) The wind whipped at his face, drawing tears
     from half closed eyes …

546) There were polka dots on one end …
547) It wasn't something to be embarrassed about …
548) It was hard to work out who needed this most …
549) I was pretty much resigned to just being
     friends …
550) She hadn't said anything about it to him …
551) It was an hour later when we realised none of
     us had paid …
552) This was the only safe place in the storm …
553) I was aware I'd crossed the line …
554) She'd never have found out if it wasn't for …
555) It wasn't what was usually posted on that
     website …
556) I didn't want to upset my friend …
557) Telling stories was her art form …
558) There was a tent in the middle of the field …
559) I'd forgotten to order cat food …
560) I'd never experienced that sort of gentleness
     before …
561) He hadn't intended to take such liberties …
562) I couldn't stop it now even if I wanted to …
563) The cows were all lying down …
564) We should have called the police at the
     beginning …
565) Yesterday was brutal …
566) I'd been up all night prepping …
567) There was fifteen minutes before he had to face
     the firing squad …
568) Nobody was ever going to believe it …
569) How was I ever supposed to believe him again …
570) I had been hoping to get past my trust issues …
571) Everyone said he got what he deserved …
572) I knew it would never get any further …
573) The jackpot counter was just an inch away …
574) I couldn't quite believe I had made it …
575) I would have taken whatever she was offering …

576) We were all on the same path …
577) There are things you know that you have no idea
     that you know …
578) It was certainly a brave move …
579) My heart shattered into a thousand pieces …
580) There was just the tiniest flicker of
     unquenchable hope left …
581) Doing almost anything else would have been
     better …
582) It felt like I was behind from the very
     beginning …
583) He made her sit down before he told her …
584) He'd always been told that dolls were for girls
     …
585) She couldn't see a way out …
586) I'd been restless all day …
587) There was only one question left …
588) I'd always wanted to go there …
589) The next act was the one everyone was waiting
     for …
590) She was looking for a spatula but instead she
     found …
591) They'd only been apart for a week …
592) The horse came back alone …
593) Whichever path he chose would ruin someone's
     life …
594) At some point we would have to learn to get
     along …
595) Everyone always told her she looked just like
     her mother …
596) The address on the envelope was hand written …
597) The observation was an astute one …
598) I wouldn't have called it a test run exactly …
599) Somebody must have seen something …
600) I was a little concerned for my ear drums …
601) I didn't know everyone was doing it …

602) She realised they needed time apart …
603) She had overwhelming urge to interrupt him …
604) He definitely wasn't the right person to ask
     for help …
605) Something about the window wasn't quite right …
606) The collar was grey and pink …
607) She wasn't sure if it was an angel or an alien
     …
608) I'd been waiting for this parcel for weeks …
609) I couldn't stop looking …
610) The best critics are always the most honest …
611) My first placement was on the gynaecology ward
     …
612) It wasn't exactly a walk in the park …
613) When he didn't reply I thought they'd got him …
614) One word would have silenced them …
615) We would all be working late after this …
616) Summer seemed a long way off …
617) Some people really do talk rubbish …
618) It really was very simple …
619) Nobody had ever escaped from an ether box
     before …
620) She was as free and wild as a wolf …
621) I was just putting the garden to bed …
622) He had always loved fried green tomatoes …
623) It was the little things that made her happy …
624) I knew I shouldn't take that short cut …
625) This would have been a good year I think …
626) They were dancing for the sheer joy of it …
627) Dolphins might be the most beautiful creatures
     in the world …
628) It seemed that one night was all I was going to
     get …
629) The volcano was definitely smoking …
630) The calf seemed reluctant to move …
631) It was brutal but it was the only way …

632) He looked over his shoulder one last time …
633) It was only a tenth of one percent …
634) We'd never had an agreement with them …
635) We needed to streamline the management team …
636) Nobody believed he could do it …
637) We couldn't crack it open …
638) An ordinary kitchen just wasn't going to cut it
       …
639) The accuracy was nothing short of miraculous …
640) My feet just wouldn't stop getting in the way …
641) There didn't seem to be any discernible pattern
       …
642) A shallow lagoon was our training ground …
643) There weren't many armies this large …
644) The fledglings tried to stay out of the water …
645) He desperately needed to up his game …
646) It was definitely time for a clear out …
647) We had to learn quickly to survive …
648) A rupture appeared in the centre of the park …
649) It was easy to see when a storm was brewing …
650) The neighbours didn't look very impressed …

Chapter 7 - In a Place Like This

Every place has its own story. Look at these brief descriptions and ask yourself what the story of that place is. Who were the people whose lives touched it? What happened to them? Use the spider diagram technique or free write until you have something that seems like a fully formed idea you can use for a story or poem. This type of prompt is equally good for poetry or prose, and can produce some powerful results. Imagine you are walking around the place and looking for clues. The more details you can add to the starting description the richer your story will be.

651) A barn with a broken weathervane, in the centre of an overgrown field
652) A canal boat, rusted and decaying in a side stream nobody has sailed down in over thirty years
653) A terraced house in the middle of a long row of similar houses, the outer walls are painted green
654) A railway crossing in a busy town centre, a red scarf is tied to the fence
655) A giant oak tree in the centre of a small wood, there is a black X painted on its trunk
656) A farm at the top of a sea cliff, chickens are scratching around the door
657) A narrow wooden pier leading far out across a clear lake
658) A bench on the river bank, partially obscured by the leaves of a tree.
659) A tiny hut nestled in the side of a hill, the door is open

660) A thatched cottage in a little village,
     climbing roses adorn the walls and there are
     window boxes full of flowers
661) A slum made of metal sheets and cardboard
     boxes, there are naked children playing in the
     dirt
662) A mountain pass leading upwards into the clouds
663) An oasis at the edge of the desert, the cold
     ashes of a camp fire lie under a palm tree
664) An abandoned oil rig in the middle of the north
     sea
665) A field containing a corn maze with a "Danger,
     No Entry" sign at the entrance
666) A street paved with bricks of black and cream
     in wavy stripes
667) A courtyard surrounded by stables containing
     well fed horses
668) A house on stilts over a marsh
669) A car work shop with tools strewn on the floor
     and a car still on the ramps
670) A log cabin in the mountains, it's empty but
     the chimney is smoking
671) A motor boat moored to a rock on the coast of a
     deserted island
672) A large and busy church in the centre of a town
     in the bible belt, singing can be heard from
     the choir room
673) A factory, all the rooms are full and all the
     machines are working, except one
674) Easter island, by a statue with a set of
     initials carved into its nose
675) A castle turret, a discarded bow and arrow on
     one side and a pile of cannon balls on the
     other
676) A garden, neatly bedded, with fifty different
     kinds of roses

677) A park, a swing on uneven chains hangs over a
     well scuffed patch of grass
678) A cliff face dotted with windows
679) A child's bedroom, a thin layer of dust lies
     over everything
680) Mud huts in the middle of the rainforest
681) A steep staircase cut into the side of a
     mountain
682) A hill with a perfectly round ridge running
     around it's crown
683) An underground chamber with intricate carvings
     inlaid with gold covering the walls
684) A ruined city that glows red when the sun sets
685) A circle of standing stones, there are four
     layers to the circle, the stones are about 3
     feet high and uncapped
686) An abandoned petrol station, the reading on the
     machine is £1.45
687) A town square with a statue of a Lion in the
     centre and a bunch of flowers tied to the iron
     railings around the statue.
688) Underneath a bridge by the canal, discarded
     beer cans litter the ground
689) A bridge that goes half way over a river and
     then stops as though nobody ever finished
     building it
690) A mini golf course in the grounds of a ruined
     castle
691) A river that forks into two around an island on
     which is built a single tower with a door but
     no windows
692) A large building in the centre of a town, one
     wall is almost completely taken up by a clock
     face, but there are no hands for the clock.

693) A red brick house surrounded by a dry stone
     wall, neatly mown lawns, and a wooden gate
     bearing the name "Hollybush House"
694) An office, every desk immaculate, every chair
     neatly pushed in, rows of identical white
     computers all facing the same way as if the
     workers were students at school.
695) A great expanse of salt water in a valley
     between three mountains permanently capped with
     snow
696) A room in a large home, there is a large,
     imposing desk and hard upright chair, on the
     wall is a painting of a knight
697) A white cottage on the banks of the river,
     trees are growing close to the building, ducks
     swim on the river
698) A graveyard so old the names on the gravestones
     have long been erased, but someone still cuts
     the grass and leaves fresh flowers on one grave
699) An orange grove, a brown terrier-type dog with
     a grey muzzle sleeps in the shade under one of
     the trees
700) A natural arch way in the desert, in one of the
     crevices in the rock is a green glass bottle,
     miraculously still intact
701) A coast line with no beach, hundreds of
     seabirds nest on the sheer cliffs, a flag flies
     at the top of the cliff
702) The bottom of the sea, diving equipment is
     strewn across the sand, tiny colourful fish
     pick at some remains
703) A crater in the centre of a grass plain, the
     plain is green but the inside of the crater is
     brown – bare.

704) Steep mountains covered in trees with rich
     green leaves that look almost like moss growing
     on small stones
705) A red rock rising high up into the sky, all
     around it are wooden walkways and small wooden
     huts
706) A clearing in a pine forest, logs are piled up
     in the centre and identical tree stumps poke
     above the ferns in neat rows
707) Sand so white it looks like snow - footprints
     wind a path through the gypsum grasses growing
     in tufts
708) A lobby with a giant slide leading down from
     the first floor to the entrance hall
709) An office where all the chairs have been
     replaced with exercise balls
710) A car show room with black tyre marks on the
     shiny floor
711) A field containing hundreds of decaying vintage
     cars, some have been there so long trees have
     grown up through the middle of them
712) A Santa's grotto in the centre of a rugby
     pitch, Santa appears to be drunk
713) A hotel with a roof top swimming pool that
     nobody ever swims in
714) A caravan site, teams of black and white horses
     are tethered by every caravan
715) A big top tent, every bench is knocked over and
     there is blood in the ring
716) A coffee shop fitted out entirely in pink rose
     patterned cushions, wallpaper and matching
     table cloths,
717) An empty cargo hold with a hole cut in the side
718) A cave with bones scattered around the entrance

719) A castle surrounded by a moat six feet deep,
     water green with algae conceals dangerous metal
     spikes
720) A road appearing to lead nowhere in particular,
     a mile marker reads 25 miles but the name of
     the town is scrubbed off
721) A field with dozens of animals sculpted from
     willow twigs arranged as if having a tea party
722) A double bed in a tunnel leading through an
     aquarium
723) An empty cell, the mattress from the iron bed
     frame ripped into small pieces
724) A crowded club, there are carpets on the stairs
     and the bars are solid marble
725) A cow byre, the roof is sagging and the door
     creaks on rusty hinges but the cows are bedded
     with deep straw and the animals are fat and
     contented
726) A round room several stories high, there are
     sofas around the edges and the walls above them
     are lined with books to the ceiling many floors
     above
727) A treehouse with a proper front door, windows
     with real glass in them and white curtains with
     green polka dots
728) A giant obstacle course in the middle of a
     forest, the wooden obstacles are twenty feet
     high
729) A rodeo ground, horses in one paddock, cows in
     another, the centre ring surrounded by stands
     worn from the stamping of thousands of feet
730) A curiosity shop full of trinkets and
     paintings, in one corner a golden teapot sits
     on an ornate welsh dresser

731) A coffee shop in a round white tent at an
     agricultural show, coffee cups and trays on
     every table but the seats are empty
732) A green house filled with exotic flowers, a
     sleek black watering can is by the door
733) A little restaurant with only two tables and
     maritime artefacts covering the walls
734) An aeroplane hanger, doors are slightly ajar
     and an RAF plane can be seen though the opening
735) A dilapidated shed hiding at the bottom of a
     vineyard, there is a path through the weeds to
     the door, which has been freshly painted with
     creosote
736) A pond around which somebody has built a fairy
     garden with wooden toadstools, miniature houses
     and animal figurines
737) A waterfall cascading down the side of a
     mountain, hiding the entrance to a tunnel into
     the centre of the mountain
738) A tulip farm with fields of many different
     colours like a patchwork quilt on the hillside
739) An open air chapel by the beach, it is
     decorated with sea shells and plastic pelicans
740) A dirt track leading to a farmhouse on the
     Northumberland moors, sheep graze on either
     side of the path
741) A lagoon, blue and clear, fed by a perfect
     semi-circle of waterfalls cascading over moss
     coloured brown rocks
742) A wood chip path leading through a forest of
     poplar trees to a bridge over a tiny stream
743) A country church at the bottom of a valley
     surrounded by fields of wheat
744) Bunk beds carved into the side of a cave, fur
     blankets covering them, an axe rests against
     the other wall

745) A hunting lodge with rabbit skins drying on a
    line outside and a pair of spaniels lying on
    the porch
746) A school gymnasium littered with discarded
    shoes and plastic cups
747) A fun fair at night, clowns are wandering
    around and there are lights flashing everywhere
748) A stately home that has fallen into disrepair,
    the windows are boarded up and there are deer
    in the garden
749) A suburban garden, there are no flower beds, a
    rabbit has dug holes in the lawn and the gravel
    desperately needs weeding
750) A bungalow that hasn't been redecorated since
    the 1970's, faded photographs hang on every
    wall and the kitchen tap hasn't worked for ten
    years

Chapter 8 – How Could This Go Wrong?

We know that a good story needs to have conflict, because without conflict there is no story, just people going about their daily lives. In our own lives it might be preferable for everything to go right, but in a book or a short story that would be boring. Think about the following situations and ask yourself – how many ways could this go wrong? What would be the worst way it could go wrong? Use the spider diagram technique if you have trouble coming up with a workable scenario, then write that story.

751) Auditioning for a TV cookery show
752) Throwing a birthday party for a two year old
753) Walking the neighbour's dog
754) Mowing the lawn
755) Buying a new television set
756) Cleaning out the attic in a parent's house
757) Walking into a pub to meet some friends
758) Going to a yoga retreat in the welsh mountains
759) Rescuing a toad from the middle of the road
760) Catching the train to work in the morning
761) Going for a run in the park
762) Putting a house on the market
763) Attending a farm auction to try and buy a tractor
764) Taking part in a clinical trial for a new anti-depressant drug
765) Planning a family holiday abroad
766) Having a picnic in the countryside
767) Hiring a rowing boat on the river in Cambridge
768) Cooking a romantic meal for a partner or potential partner

769) Taking singing lessons
770) Going on a date with someone met online
771) Trying to rob a bank
772) Last minute Christmas shopping
773) Driving home in the dark
774) Visiting the natural history museum
775) Going to an exhibition opening at an art
     gallery
776) Going to church on a Sunday morning
777) Attending a protest march in a capital city
778) Running a marathon for the first time
779) Making a voodoo doll
780) Setting up a nanny cam in the living room
781) Going to the job centre to claim jobseekers
     allowance
782) Applying for planning permission to build an
     extension on a house
783) The funeral of a family member
784) Revealing that someone in the family supports
     the "wrong" football team
785) Playing in a poker tournament
786) Recording a short film for a school project
787) Bringing home a new pet from a rescue centre
788) Hiking up a mountain
789) Taking the kids out for a bike ride
790) Going for lunch with a close friend
791) Attending your first ever ballet class
792) Taking an important exam
793) Someone's first driving lesson
794) Looking for a nursing home for a parent with
     dementia
795) Going swimming at the local pool
796) Telling a child they're adopted
797) A camp out in the forest
798) Climbing a wall at the indoor pursuits centre
799) A golden wedding anniversary party

800) Building a treehouse
801) Painting a fence
802) A trip to the zoo
803) A guided tour around the pyramids in Egypt
804) A new job driving for a wealthy business man
805) Hunting for unicorns in the garden
806) Reading a story to a child
807) Attending a conference relating to work
808) A hen do in a Scottish castle
809) A Halloween trip to a haunted house
810) Going swimming in the sea
811) A road trip with a college friend
812) Miniature golf with the family
813) Throwing a surprise party for your Dad
814) Buying a lucky charm from a craft fair
815) Taking a puppy to training classes
816) A day out at an agricultural show
817) An office baking competition
818) Hiring a new window cleaner
819) Placing a lonely hearts ad
820) Following a high school sweetheart to
     university
821) Going on safari
822) Studying viruses to find a cure for cancer
823) Walking out of your own front door at just the
     wrong time
824) Arriving late to the office Christmas party
825) Answering your phone without looking at the
     caller ID first
826) Having three students with the same name in one
     class
827) A group assignment at school or university
828) Trying to jump start a tractor
829) Setting traps for the moles digging up a garden
830) Designing new uniforms for the staff at a café
     to wear

831) Planning a wedding without telling the couple
     anything about it
832) Finding a £50 note
833) Taking part in a mountain biking challenge
834) Leaving the house without your mobile phone
835) Leaving Dad in charge of the kids at home
836) Buying new school clothes for a teenage girl
837) Appearing on a TV talent show
838) Dating someone obsessed with cats
839) Putting up a new garden fence
840) Playing a board game
841) Visiting the principal's office/boss's office
842) Hanging out the washing on a clothes line
843) Drinking wine with friends
844) Checking a book out of the library
845) A school trip
846) Joining a class at the gym
847) Taking a horse to a gymkhana
848) Trying to rescue a princess
849) Exploring an abandoned house
850) Hunting for frogspawn

Chapter 9 - Write About This

Sometimes you just need something to write about.
What we don't realise is that we have thousands of
things to write about every single day. All we have
to do is tap into the endless resources around us
and the stories will jump out at us. Use the
following prompts to write about the world around
you. Let story ideas flow on to the page as you
observe, or recall your observations. Set the timer
for as long as you find comfortable and free write.

851) The view from your window
852) How you met a childhood friend
853) The last person you sat next to on the bus
854) The cashier that served you last time you went
     to the supermarket
855) The homeless person on your local high street
856) The location where your favourite TV show is
     filmed
857) The last news story that popped up on your
     social media account
858) The last place you went on holiday
859) A minor character in the last book you read
860) How you came to own your pet
861) The last dream you remember
862) The last time you felt afraid
863) The last sad story a friend told you
864) The last time you felt angry on someone else's
     behalf
865) Someone you don't know walking past your office
866) A stranger's tattoo
867) The fish in the nearest body of water to you
868) The results of a competition you don't
     particularly care about

869) What happens when Jehovah's witnesses knock at
     your door
870) The picture on the front of the nearest cereal
     box
871) The last person you saw getting drunk
872) A crime that affected you personally
873) Your zombie apocalypse escape plan
874) A secret bunker in your garden
875) An embarrassing secret you wouldn't want anyone
     to know
876) The most interesting cupboard under the stairs
     you can think of
877) An item in a display cabinet
878) A photograph on someone's fridge
879) A person you were afraid of
880) The person with the wildest hair style you have
     ever seen
881) The biggest festival or event in your home town
882) What you would do if you won the lottery
883) A stretch of road near where you live where a
     lot of crashes happen
884) A path you have always wondered where it leads
885) A person from another culture you met recently
886) Someone you love deeply
887) A painting that hangs on the wall of a
     relative's home
888) A horse trotting down the road where you live
889) A bird that flew into your window
890) The ants winding their way across the patio in
     someone's back garden
891) The last time you made the wrong decision
892) An argument online
893) Something that makes your stomach churn
894) A television advert that told a story
895) A dead end
896) An experience of rejection

897) A series of minor problems occurring all at
     once
898) The mincepie maverick
899) The most cluttered room in the house
900) Knocking at an important door
901) Setting a fire
902) Being right about something you would rather
     you were wrong about
903) Making a plan
904) Someone whose calls you always answer
905) Someone whose calls you never answer
906) A time when you needed back up
907) The worst place your phone could ring
908) Someone playing the piano
909) A weekend that was supposed to be restful
910) A photograph that disturbed you
911) Something you should have been able to predict
912) A new neighbour
913) Throwing something
914) Feeling like you're jumping through hoops
915) Something extremely disorganised
916) A process of elimination
917) A face that doesn't fit
918) Something you couldn't put down
919) Travelling at a high speed
920) An unusual type of school
921) Something you want to get back
922) Someone else's presentation
923) A death that could have been presented
924) Something that embarrassed a grandparent
925) Something the neighbours didn't see
926) An act of remorse
927) A reason to go to church
928) Someone who refuses to go to church
929) The home life of someone you only know in a
     professional capacity

930) The price behind something free
931) Expectations of happiness
932) How something that causes pain can be managed
933) A journey that never seems to end
934) A person that makes your chest feel tight when
    you think about them
935) An impressive thing a friend has done recently
936) The reason why someone hasn't moved a used
    coffee mug
937) A problem that the next person you see might be
    hiding
938) A mistake on a sign in the street
939) A minor suggestion that changed someone's life
940) What happened last time you played a board game

Chapter 10 – Finish the Story

Sometimes you need a little bit more than just a few words to help you think of a story. Sometimes you actually need to have the story started for you. Sometimes it's not that you need to have the story started for you but just that you enjoy writing to finish a scenario that someone has randomly thrown at you. Whichever is true for you the following prompts give you just that. Stories which already have a beginning. All you have to do is decide where to go from here. There are of course an infinite number of possibilities for each scenario, but only one of them will be the story *you* have to tell.

941) An old letter is found inside the drawer of an antique desk
942) In a small town a young girl steps on to the train tracks
943) A thug for hire is contracted to steal a briefcase - but he steals the wrong one
944) A girl with multi coloured hair steps into the back of a taxi
945) A dog out on a walk discovers a garbage bag and starts to scratch at it
946) A family return home to find their house has been burgled, but only one item has been taken
947) A stowaway is discovered on board an aeroplane
948) Someone misses the train to work
949) A storm blows down an old tree, the workmen sent to remove it discover something buried between the roots
950) Someone discovers they are not alone in their house

951) A child drops their favourite teddy bear off a
     bridge
952) A phone rings in an important meeting
953) A old man realises his new neighbour is his
     high school sweetheart from many decades ago
954) The police break down a door
955) On a lonely little-travelled road, a dog is
     thrown from the back of a van
956) A letter informing someone they have an
     interview for a job goes astray in the mail
957) A magician is booked to appear at a children's
     party
958) A bird appears at a window in a city centre
     school
959) A key that had been lost for a long time is
     found tucked inside an old shoe
960) A man withdraws £5000 cash from his bank
     account
961) An animal is rescued from a river
962) A woman sees someone she used to know on TV
963) A girl gallops through the night on the back of
     a horse
964) A child stumbles on a portal to a magical world
965) Someone picks up a book from the library and
     discovers the first and last pages have been
     torn out
966) A new employee is called into the boss's office
     on their first day
967) A dragon lands on your roof
968) An audience sit down to enjoy a play at a
     renowned theatre
969) Somewhere nearby someone fires a gun
970) You find a knife under your room-mate's pillow
971) A 'for sale' sign goes up outside a neighbour's
     house

972) A colleague fails to turn up for work, nobody
     can get hold of them on the phone
973) You get a new postman
974) Someone is stung by a bee
975) Four youngsters go into a nightclub. Only three
     will come out.
976) The devil himself shows up at someone's bedside
977) A bin is knocked over by a pair of cats
     fighting
978) A car crashes through a brick wall into a busy
     market square
979) A man sits at his kitchen table crying, in his
     hand is a letter
980) A mirror is broken in a hotel bathroom
981) From an attic room nobody has been in for years
     there comes a knocking
982) A scathing review of a restaurant appears in a
     local newspaper
983) A child is sent to live with their grandparents
     for the summer
984) Someone discovers a map that seems to change by
     itself
985) Someone finds an old recipe book
986) A bird flies into a window
987) A boy on a skateboard takes a misstep and
     skates into the middle of a busy road
988) A witch casts a spell, only she got an
     ingredient wrong in the potion
989) Someone makes a crucial mistake inside a power
     station
990) A set of divorce papers are pushed through a
     letter box
991) A man waits nervously at the alter
992) A newly turned vampire awakes for the first
     time
993) A rabbit is caught in a trap

994) A very old person decides to throw themselves a
     birthday party
995) Something or someone escapes from the circus
996) An entire village vanishes overnight
997) Two young people meet, and hate each other on
     sight
998) Someone orders a pint of a very specific local
     beer at a bar
999) Someone responds to an ad in the paper for an
     odd job man at a stately home
1000)   Four college friends plan a road trip
     across Europe
1001)   A circle of standing stones begin to move

<u>Also available by Sarah Hindmarsh</u>

The Animal Adventures Series

'The Mouse Who Howled at the Moon'
'The Squirrel Who Travelled the World'
'The Squirrel Who Adventured with Otters'
'The Lizard Who Drank the Rain'

The 1001 Writing Prompts Series

'1001 Writing Prompts for Generating Ideas'
'1001 Writing Prompts for Character Development'
'1001 More Writing Prompts for Generating Ideas'

About the Author

Sarah Hindmarsh is an administrator working in Lincolnshire, where she lives with her miniature poodle Kohla. 'The Squirrel who Sailed to Adventure' is the fifth book in the Animal Adventures series. Sarah also writes books for writers. '1001 Writing Prompts for Generating Ideas' and '1001 Writing Prompts for character development' are available for kindle now. In her spare time Sarah enjoys horse riding, walking her dog and playing rugby. She is also a keen biologist and finds much of her inspiration in the natural world.

Sarah writes a blog centred on engaging children with reading at http://creatingwithkohla.com, you can also follow her on Twitter @creating_kohla and find her on Facebook by searching for Creating With Kohla. The blog and website contain resources for parents, teachers and home schoolers as well as free to read stories and poems and updates about upcoming work.